P9-DBP-383

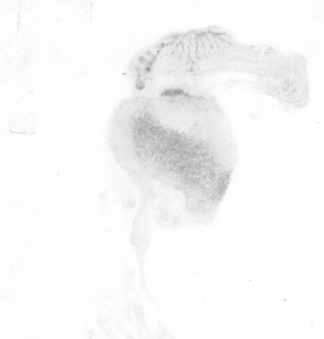

THE FREEDOM OF SPEECH IN AMERICA

The IN AMERICA *Series*

THE FREEDOM OF SPEECH IN AMERICA

RAVINA GELFAND

Published by
Lerner Publications Company
Minneapolis, Minnesota

The author wishes to express her gratitude for the assistance so graciously and unsparingly given by William B. Lockhart, Dean and Professor of Law, University of Minnesota, and J. Edward Gerald, Professor of Journalism, University of Minnesota.

. . . CONTENTS . . .

Viet Nam peace march, New York City, April 1967. In a democracy, freedom of speech enables the individual to express his opinions and the government to know what the citizens want.

Patrick Henry delivers an attack upon King George III and the Stamp Act. Virginia Assembly, 1765.

PART I

What Do We Mean by Free Speech?

1. *How the Words Are Used Today*

The phrase "freedom of speech" means the freedom to express ideas. It is the freedom which allows us to criticize any government official, from the President of the United States to the local game warden. It is the freedom to try to change people's minds. This means we can disagree with accepted ideas, including highly respected ideas about religion, science, and government. It is the freedom to try to convince others to accept a new way of thinking.

When you hear the words "freedom of speech," you probably think of the right to *talk* freely. However, the term often includes more than just speechmaking, but any of the ways used by man to publicly present his ideas. These ideas may be published in newspapers, magazines, and books. They may be spoken or acted in plays, movies, and television, or broadcast on the radio.

2. *The Most Personal Ways to Present Ideas*

This book will discuss only three of the ways in which speech is used publicly to present ideas — by talking directly to an individual or group, by handing out pamphlets or handbills, and by carrying a protest sign. These are among the most personal and direct ways the average person can use the right of free speech. Books, newspapers, and magazines have publishers and editors to decide what will and what will not be printed. Radio and television programs have sponsors and program directors who decide what should be broadcast. Plays and movies are influenced by their financial backers, producers, and directors. But no money is needed by a person desiring to make a speech or carry a protest sign. The speaker alone decides what he wants to say. Handbills, too, are a popular way to express ideas. They can be produced easily and cheaply, and so are widely used by individuals or groups with little money.

Conversation with an individual or a group is one of the simplest ways to exercise the right of free speech.

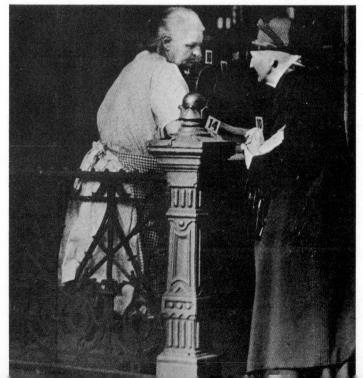

The Bill of Rights first appeared as a joint resolution of Congress in 1789. Ten of the 12 suggested amendments were ratified by the states and became part of the Constitution in 1791.

3. *How Free Do We Want Speech to Be?*

Experience has taught us the importance of freedom of speech. Without it many new ideas would not be heard. If speech were not free we could have no democracy. Men could not criticize unjust laws and work to get them changed. There would be no use in holding elections if we could not hear the beliefs of all candidates. Freedom of speech is a right which protects all other rights. Yet, how free do we want speech to be?

Freedom of speech became a part of the Constitution of the United States on December 15, 1791 when the First Amendment was ratified. This amendment, one of ten included in the Bill of Rights, states that:

Congress shall make no law respecting an establishment of religion, or prohibiting the free exercise thereof; or abridging the freedom of speech, or of the press; or of the rights of the people peaceably to assemble, and to petition the Government for a redress of grievances.

Although the amendment clearly states that Congress shall make no law restricting the freedom of speech, there are such laws. Was the First Amendment intended to be an absolute guarantee that government had no power to limit speech in any way? Some people believe so. However, most people feel that there must be some limits on freedom of speech. What should the limits be?

Think about how free you want speech to be. History has shown that how much or how little freedom of speech America has is influenced by the wishes of its citizens.

The right to carry a protest sign is protected by the First Amendment.

4. The Problem of Setting Limits

It is not easy to decide how free we want speech to be. What about people who use speech to spread hatred? Should a man be allowed to use a public park to attack Negroes, Jews, Catholics, or any other race or religion he happens to dislike? Our belief in freedom of speech is truly put to the test when we hear people expressing ideas with which we strongly disagree. A few states have laws prohibiting "hate peddling," but most do not. Some people feel there should be such laws in every state. Their argument is this: under the laws of libel and slander, it is a crime to say or write something that is damaging to the reputation of an individual. Therefore, why is it any less a crime to say something damaging about a group?

Others feel that free speech must be free for everyone, even those whose ideas are sickening to most Americans. They believe that no ideas are safe if government can dictate which ideas are acceptable and which are not. Let the hate peddlers speak, they say, and let others tell a different side of the story — the people will know who is telling the truth.

Minneapolis students demand that drivers recognize their right to have a crosswalk.

What about words which might be dangerous? Should they be permitted in the name of free speech? The man in a crowded jet who thinks it is a joke to cry out, "There is a bomb on this plane," is using speech that is dangerous and most people would feel that he should be arrested.

What about a man making a speech to a group of antiwar demonstrators in a public park? Some soldiers strolling through the park stop to hear what the man is saying. "Anyone who fights in a war is a murderer," he says. This man's speech could very well start a fight among the members of the audience. But what if the speaker has no intention of causing trouble and is merely expressing his ideas? If trouble does threaten, who should be removed from the park — the speaker or the members of the audience who want to stop him from speaking? Did the speaker use "fighting words" — expressions so insulting to his listeners that they refuse to accept them in silence? Are such words a part of free speech?

Three things can help us decide how free we want speech to be: 1) understanding the past; 2) knowing the reasons for freedom of speech and the reasons given for limiting such freedom; 3) thinking about how much freedom of speech will best make the America of the future the kind of nation we want it to be.

PART II

A Glimpse Into the Past

Seldom in the history of the world have conditions been right for the idea of free speech to be accepted. The thought that free speech should include the right to criticize one's government hardly existed until sometime after America became a nation. Before freedom of speech became part of the Constitution of the United States, few ordinary citizens could speak out against their government without fear of punishment. But ideas about free speech do have a long history.

In the fourth and fifth centuries B.C., the citizens of Athens loved and respected freedom. Their city-state was one of the earliest democracies. Yet, the people of Athens tried to silence one of their great men, the philosopher Socrates. When he refused to be silenced he was tried and executed. Socrates had spent his life questioning and criticizing the beliefs and conduct of his fellow citizens. This angered many people who did not care to be ridiculed by Socrates' questions and remarks. Finally these people found a way to stop Socrates' use of free speech. They could not get rid of him for his criticism of themselves, but they accused him of corrupting the youth of the city and also of dishonor and impiety toward the gods.

Almost all societies have held the latter two actions to be crimes. Each society tries to protect its children and its sacred beliefs. Socrates denied the accusations and made several speeches defending his conduct. He tried to show that he had only sought truth and meant no dishonor to the gods. He was condemned to death, however, and although he could have escaped he refused to do so.

He died after drinking a cup of poisonous hemlock, the ancient Greek way of execution.

The martyrdom of Socrates is only one famous instance of a man who sacrificed his life for the right to speak freely. History gives many sad examples of men who suffered because they sought to criticize their government, or the religious authorities of their time. The great Italian astronomer, Galileo, was silenced by the church leaders of his day. The Roman Catholic Church then believed that the earth was the center of the universe. Galileo taught that the earth is not the center of the universe, and that the earth revolves around the sun. Church leaders forced Galileo to deny his own beliefs.

Socrates (469?-399 B. C.). By questioning the beliefs of other Athenians, he tried to demonstrate the difference between opinion and knowledge.

Martin Luther (1483-1546) refused to recant, or deny beliefs that conflicted with the Roman Catholic Church. Although he was excommunicated by the Pope, Luther himself was not tolerant of other Protestants who disagreed with him.

Religious authorities, whatever their views, have often sought to silence those who disagreed with them. Martin Luther broke with the Roman Catholic Church. When Lutheranism became a state religion, however, it did not allow freedom of speech and conscience to all men. The Puritans fled from persecution in England and settled in America so that they would have freedom to worship according to their conscience. But when a Puritan minister, Roger Williams, criticized his church's leaders, they expelled him from the Massachusetts Bay Colony. Williams then founded Rhode Island, where complete religious toleration was granted to all people.

Roger Williams arrives in Rhode Island, 1636.

The Constitutional Convention met in Philadelphia during the summer of 1787. The delegates had planned to revise the weak Articles of Confederation; instead, they drew up a new framework for government. Some states felt that the Constitution was not complete without a guarantee of individual liberties, and hesitated to ratify. In 1789 James Madison, one of the chief authors of the Constitution, drew up a list of amendments which became the Bill of Rights.

Religious tolerance and freedom of speech are closely related. Only where the former exists, can the latter also exist. The framers of the Bill of Rights knew this and purposely included freedom of speech and religion in the same amendment. They wanted to create an American nation which would guarantee its citizens more freedom than man had previously had in society: freedom of conscience, of conduct, and of speech.

PART III

Speech Under English Rule

1. *England's Influence on the American Constitution*

As the founding fathers of this nation worked out their plans for the American Constitution and Bill of Rights, they kept in mind the law and history of England. They wanted this nation to benefit from all the struggles for freedom that had been won in England plus a special American kind of freedom which would make each person someone of value in his own right.

The long battle for freedom of speech in England was mainly a striving to speak without fear on two matters — religion and political affairs. The struggle for freedom of opinion on religious matters is part of the whole story of religious persecution and is a history in itself.

2. *Why Political Discussion Was Suppressed*

Two reasons were used to stop any discussion of political affairs. One of these was the belief among rulers that what government did was no business of the people. The people, it was said, had nothing to do with the laws but to obey them. The second reason is still used today: the belief that criticism of the government, its laws, or its leaders weakens the government and thereby creates danger for the entire society.

Queen Elizabeth (1533-1603). The Tudors generally dominated their Parliaments with ease, but late in the century, when Elizabeth's popularity was waning, she found it necessary to limit the members' freedom of speech.

3. *The Struggle to Debate Issues in Parliament*

Speech in England during the sixteenth and seventeenth centuries was so restricted that even members of Parliament could not debate the issues they were to vote on. When they asked Queen Elizabeth in 1593 to allow debate on the floor of Parliament, she replied: "Privilege of speech is granted, but you must know what privilege you have; not to speak every one what he listeth, or what cometh in his brain to utter that; but your privilege is Aye or No." In other words, the Queen told them that their freedom of speech consisted only of the right to vote yes or no on legislation.

King James I, who succeeded Elizabeth as ruler of England, felt so strongly about citizens speaking out on political affairs that he issued a proclamation against "excesse of lavish and licentious speech on matters of state." Freedom of speech, said the King, didn't extend to matters of state which were "no theames, or subjects fit for vulgar persons, or common meetings . . . ." James ordered anyone who heard an Englishman discussing public affairs to report that person within 24 hours or be sent to prison. So far as the King was concerned, anyone who didn't report such a crime was as guilty as the one committing it.

James, like Elizabeth before him, refused to let Parliament debate issues. Again, members of Parliament protested their lack of freedom of discussion. But they wanted free speech only for themselves. The very year of their protest against King James, they tried an old man named Floyd for the crime of talking objectionably in the streets of London. Floyd's crime was that he had questioned the right of James' son-in-law to be King of Bohemia and said that he was happy that this prince had been defeated in a battle. Floyd declared that he hadn't said these things at all, but few cared about his claim of innocence. Members of Parliament were so horrified that a citizen would criticize the royal family in public, they tried to outdo each other in thinking up punishment severe enough for the old man. "Let his tongue be cut off!" they shouted during his trial. "Let him be branded on the forehead! Let his nose and ears be lopped off!"

4. *Suppression by Licensing*

When members of Parliament finally won the freedom to debate issues in 1689, they reserved this right for themselves. Although the English were a freedom-loving people and were gradually gaining many liberties, the idea that men should be able to publicly criticize their governments made slow progress.

The main control of political criticism in England during the sixteenth and seventeenth centuries was the licensing of printed materials. When Johann Gutenberg invented printing from movable type in 1450, church officials immediately ruled that nothing could be printed which was not licensed. Licensing meant that all materials had to be approved by an official reader, or censor, before they could be printed. Censorship by licensing continued until the end of the seventeenth century.

Johann Gutenberg (1395-1468) invented printing from movable type. This uniform metal type, made in molds, could be pulled apart and reset for new pages. For the first time, it was possible to print many copies of a single book.

But the printing press had given man a new way to express his thoughts, and a man with an idea bursting inside of him is not likely to keep it to himself. Men took to writing their hopes for society, their thoughts on religion and politics, and their protests against certain laws. They published their own works in pamphlets.

The pamphlets which flooded seventeenth century England were the subject of conversation wherever people gathered. Men and women learned how to read in order not to be left out of the lively discussions.

Nothing printed which contained criticism of the government

An English coffeehouse, about 1690. Coffee-drinking was new in seventeenth century England, and it drew people together for lively discussions.

could be licensed, but secret presses kept springing up to print unlicensed pamphlets. Men using made-up names or writing anonymously risked severe punishment as they had their pamphlets printed on illegal presses. When the crowd gathered to discuss a pamphlet it was almost certain not to be a licensed one — which was tame and dull compared to those put out on the secret presses.

5. *The First Englishmen Write About Free Speech*

Two thousand years had passed since Socrates spoke of the importance of free speech when a few men again took up the cry for liberty of expression. The best known of these men, the poet John Milton, was an active seventeenth century pamphleteer. In a pamphlet written in 1644 to attack licensing of printing, Milton wrote about freedom of the mind.

We need not be afraid to let false ideas be heard, Milton wrote, because when both true and false ideas are heard, truth will win out. (Do you think this is true?) Milton said that when someone has the power to stop some ideas from being heard, they probably would stop the true ideas even if they thought they were stopping false ones. He explained that we accept ideas to which we are accustomed without really looking at them. When someone presents an idea that makes our way of thinking about something seem false, we usually feel that it must be the new idea which is false.

. . . If it comes to prohibiting, there is not aught more likely to be prohibited than truth itself; whose first appearance to our eyes bleared and dimmed with prejudice and custom is more unsightly and unplausible than many errors. . . .

The words of John Milton, like the words of Socrates, were ideas about freedom of speech born in times not ready for them. Although his pamphlet is often quoted today, few people in Milton's time took notice of it. Licensing of printing, which Milton was protesting, continued for another half century in England. In colonial America, printing was strictly controlled long after the English licensing law no longer existed.

John Milton's greatest political pamphlet was the *Areopagitica*, his defense of a free press. It appeared in 1644, unlicensed and without the name of the printer. The Licensing Act was not terminated by Parliament until 1695, and then because it was considered impractical.

Angry groups of colonists gather to discuss and protest the British Stamp Act. Boston, 1765.

6. *Suppression by Seditious Libel Law*

The end of censorship in England in the last years of the seventeenth century, and later in colonial America, did not mean that men could now criticize the government. The law of seditious libel made it a crime to print or say anthing intended to hurt the good standing of the king or the government. No one could tell a man beforehand what he could or could not say or write. However, after the speech was made or the words were printed, the man could be punished for what he said or wrote. As late as the eighteenth century men were being imprisoned, fined, and whipped for writing what today would be considered ordinary political discussion. For many years criticism of the government which was true was as punishable as criticism that was false. In fact, at one time criticism which was true was considered more damaging, and therefore a greater crime.

7. *Free Speech at the Time of the Revolution*

By the time of the American Revolution, there was still no guaranteed freedom of speech for English subjects. In spite of this, lively political discussions were engaged in by both the people in England and the colonists in America. Prior censorship, the censoring of printed or spoken words *before* they are printed or spoken, was a thing of the past. But the speaker or writer who used words that might injure the dignity or reputation of the government could be punished after the speech was made or the written material was printed. In colonial America, the popularly elected assemblies were harder on their critics than were the representatives of the English Government.

PART IV

Freedom of Opinion in America —1791 to 1925

1. *Rights as an American Ideal*

For some colonial Americans, the Revolutionary War was fought to establish an independent nation which would grant the colonists the rights that Englishmen had already won.

Others, such as James Madison and Thomas Jefferson, dreamed of a country where, for the first time, men could enjoy liberty and justice as rights which did not have to be *given to them* by government.

Jefferson wrote in the Declaration of Independence:

We hold these truths to be self-evident, that all men are created equal, that they are endowed by their Creator with certain unalienable Rights, that among these are Life, Liberty and the pursuit of Happiness. That to secure these rights, Governments are instituted among Men, deriving their just powers from the consent of the governed. . . .

This was the basis on which the Government of the United States was formed. Other governments had persecuted men, but the United States was created to protect its citizens. For many leaders of the new republic, this was not enough. They wanted more than to be protected by government — they wanted protection from the government. Several of the states did not want to ratify the new Constitution because it did not list the basic rights and liberties which the new government could not take away.

They ratified only on condition that the Constitution be immediately amended. Ten of the amendments, as drafted by James Madison, were adopted in 1791. They are the Bill of Rights—a guarantee by law of more freedom than men anywhere had ever known.

2. *What the Nation's Founders Meant by Freedom of Speech*

The First Amendment to the Constitution was only the beginning of a new history of freedom of speech. The statement "Congress shall make no law . . . abridging the freedom of speech . . ." was accepted without question. Everyone recognized that the new nation could only succeed in being a government of the people if its citizens were free to believe what they chose and to say what they believed.

While other amendments were debated, no arguments were held on the subject of free speech. The events of history have proved, however, that to some Americans the words "Congress shall make no law" meant only that Congress shall make no law that wasn't traditionally accepted as a proper regulation of speech. To others, such as James Madison, no law meant *no law*.

3. *The Sedition Act: An Attempt to Stop Political Criticism*

Seven years after the First Amendment was adopted, Americans were forced to think about the meaning of the First Amendment's guarantee of free speech.

Ours was a country in the process of building a new form of government. It was led by outstanding men who had very different ideas about the best way for the young nation to be governed. On one side were such great patriots as George Washington, Alexander Hamilton, and John Adams of the Federalist party. On the other side were Thomas Jefferson and his Republicans (the party that later became the Democratic party).

The First Amendment met its initial test during an undeclared naval war with France, in 1798. Despite pressure from other Federalists, President Adams carefully avoided war, but he permitted American ships to attack French privateers. Above, the 20-gun *Delaware* captures the French ship *La Croyable*. Hostilities ended when the United States negotiated a treaty with Napoleon in 1799.

The differences between the Federalists and the Republicans grew more serious in 1798 when America was fighting an undeclared war with France. The Federalists believed that the Republicans were French sympathizers. John Adams was then President, and Jefferson was Vice-President. Everyone was thinking ahead to the election of 1800. Thomas Jefferson would surely head the Republican ticket for the office of President. The Federalists were worried. Jefferson's supporters were making speeches and writing newspaper articles that contained vicious attacks against the Federalists.

The Federalists asked themselves what kind of speech was protected by the First Amendment. Surely not the abuse that was being poured out against them by the Republicans. They then introduced the Sedition Act of 1798.

The Sedition Act sounded much like the English law of seditious libel. Part of the act made it a crime to write, print, or speak any false, scandalous, and malicious criticism of the President, Congress, or Government of the United States with the intention of harming their reputation or "to incite against them the hatred of the good people of the United States."

Now the debates that were missing when the First Amendment was passed began to rage.

"This will mean the end of all political discussion," the Republicans charged.

"Not so," claimed the Federalists. "The act does not censor anything spoken or written before it is said or printed. Furthermore, it only punishes false, scandalous, and malicious criticism of the President, Congress, or government."

Thomas Jefferson (1743-1824). Belief in freedom of expression was at the heart of his major actions and words: "I tolerate with the utmost latitude the right of others to differ with me in opinion." (Bust by Houdon; courtesy, Museum of Fine Arts, Boston)

James Madison (1751-1836). The Kentucky and Virginia Resolutions were written by Jefferson and Madison, respectively, in angry protest against the Sedition Act.

"Offensive criticism against the government will always be judged false," the Republicans answered. "People will be afraid to speak or write what they believe to be true. How can they possibly prove the truth of political charges to a judge and jury?"

In spite of all the arguments against the Sedition Act, it was passed by the Federalist majority in Congress. Both Thomas Jefferson and James Madison drafted resolutions of protest.

The resolution drafted by Madison said, in part, that the Sedition Act exercised . . . "a power not delegated by the Constitution, but on the contrary, expressly and positively forbidden by one of the amendments thereto — a power which, more than any other, ought to produce universal alarm, because it is levelled against the right of freely examining public characters and measures, and of free communication among the people thereon, which has ever been justly deemed the only effectual guardian of every other right."

The first person jailed under the act was Congressman Matthew Lyon of Vermont. Soon, two dozen others were arrested — all Republicans. Ten of them went to jail. Jefferson won the election of 1800. As soon as he became President, he pardoned all who had been convicted. In 1801 the Sedition Act expired.

Thomas Jefferson's belief in free speech was so strong that he spoke of it in his first inaugural address, saying that if anyone wanted to dissolve the Government of the United States, or change its form, they could speak freely. He had faith that the American people knew that this form of government was what they wanted and could not be fooled simply by hearing someone speak against it.

The passage of the Sedition Act forced the American people to think about free speech and to decide what limits they wanted on political criticism. From this experience a new idea became part of the American understanding of freedom of speech: Americans must have the broadest freedom to critize their government, their public officials, and candidates for office.

4. A Century of Free Speech

For the next 100 years freedom of speech was accepted and enjoyed. During the War of 1812, when a strong political party in New England spoke out and worked against the war effort, President James Madison refused all appeals to silence the critics. Even when scandalous attacks were made upon Madison's own reputation, and when some citizens feared that the nation would be destroyed, Madison insisted on each man's right to free speech.

During the Civil War, although there were some arrests for conspiring to overthrow the government, speech was so free that an open election could be held. Candidates hurled vigorous criticism against one another. Try to imagine any country today where a free election, with public debate of the issues, could be held during a civil war and you will get some idea of the freedom of speech our ancestors enjoyed during Lincoln's time.

Town Meeting.

Vigorous political criticism
was freely expressed in
nineteenth century America. (Below) *Politics in an
Oysterhouse*, 1848.

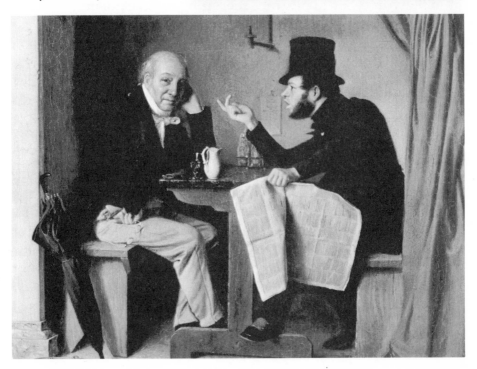

5. *The Effect of World War I*

The United States' entry into World War I brought an end to the time of taking free speech for granted. As a result of two laws passed during the war, Americans found out what can happen when enough people think it necessary to suppress liberty "just a little."

Slightly more than a month after the United States entered the war against Germany, Congress enacted the Selective Service Act (the draft) to raise an army. The majority of the people thought that the draft was necessary and fair, but there were some who protested against it. In 1917 an Espionage Act was passed which contained a section to insure no interference with the war effort or with the drafting or enlistment of men into the service. Part of this act made it a crime to speak or write false reports or statements with the intention of interfering with the operation or success of the military or naval forces, or to cause disloyalty or refusal of military duty, or to obstruct recruiting or enlistment.

The Attorney General of the United States felt that the Espionage Act worked well against planned or organized opposition by disloyal groups, but he didn't think that this was quite enough. To stop individual citizens from saying things which might hurt the war effort, he asked Congress for an amendment to the Espionage Act. At the same time, Congress was hearing from angry citizens who insisted that people criticizing the war or draft be silenced. Congress then passed the Sedition Act of 1918.

The 1918 Act made it a crime, during wartime, to say, print, write, or publish anything disloyal, profane, or abusive about the form of government of the United States, or the flag, or the uniform of the Army or Navy. It became a crime to use any word or act favoring the cause of any country at war with us. It became a crime to give disloyal advice with intent to obstruct the sale of United States bonds. When Congress passed the Sedition Act, some of the state legislatures passed espionage and sedition acts of their own.

The Sedition Act represented the will of many of the people. The United States was at war, and war is a dangerous and serious business. The supporters of the Sedition Act were good people and good citizens who loved America. They thought they were helping save their country by prohibiting the opinions of dangerous and disloyal people.

The political atmosphere of 1918 is suggested by these posters, which plead for unquestioning patriotism. Congress passed the Sedition Act because of fear that criticism might hurt the war effort. *(Posters courtesy of the Chicago Historical Society)*

But the Sedition Act turned out to be a danger in itself. People were jailed for saying things that today would be considered mere discussion. One man was arrested for saying that we should raise taxes instead of selling war bonds. Criticism of the Red Cross or YMCA led to arrest. In Minnesota, police picked up a man for telling some women that no soldier would ever see the socks they were knitting. Anyone arguing about the war in any public place — a hotel lobby, a restaurant, a train — might find himself under arrest for using language that someone considered disloyal. A farmer was arrested as a result of a conversation in his own home with two strangers he had invited to dinner when they had knocked on his door after running out of gasoline.

In all, about 2,000 people were jailed under the 1917 and 1918 laws. The law said that the intention of the words spoken or written had to be to hurt the war effort. But the men and women of the juries were in no mood to give the benefit of the doubt to the speaker. Week after week Americans read about men and women who had been convicted for making statements that might harm the war effort.

An alien is fingerprinted by a policeman, 1917. During World War I police departments kept files of information on foreign-born residents. These were years of social unrest and revolution in many parts of the world, and aliens were often assumed to be harboring dangerous ideas.

Roger N. Baldwin, principal founder of the American Civil Liberties Union. The ACLU was organized in 1920 to expand the work of the wartime National Civil Liberties Board. By means of legal aid and public information the ACLU has worked to protect the civil liberties of all Americans.

The United States had gone into World War I with no official position on free speech in wartime. As the number of arrests grew larger, the question was on everyone's mind. A civil liberties organization was founded by a group of citizens who thought the Bill of Rights was being disregarded.

Before this the Supreme Court had scarcely been involved in matters concerning free speech. Now appeals from some of the people prosecuted under the wartime laws began to come to the higher courts. Some of them reached the Supreme Court.

The first case decided by the high court was an appeal by a man named Schenck who had been found guilty of plotting to cause insubordination (disobedience) in the armed forces and of attempting to interfere with the raising of the army. Schenck had distributed circulars to men about to be drafted, calling the draft unconstitutional and saying that a draftee is "little better than a

Jane Addams, social worker and founder of Hull House, was an early member of the American Civil Liberties Union. The membership of the ACLU, then as now, represented many vocations and a wide range of political beliefs.

convict." Stating that the draft was a wrong against humanity in the interest of Wall Street's chosen few, the writer of the circular told men to assert their rights not to be drafted.

Schenck asked the Supreme Court to reverse his conviction, claiming it was a violation of his right to free speech. But a unanimous Court upheld Schenck's conviction. The opinion of the Court, written by Justice Oliver Wendell Holmes, Jr., put on record some of the Supreme Court's ideas about the constitutional protection of speech. One of those ideas is that words which are protected by the right to free speech under some circumstances, cannot be protected under other circumstances if those same words become dangerous. As an example, Justice Holmes pointed out that freedom of speech does not give a man the right to falsely shout "fire" in a theater and cause a panic.

In the words of Justice Holmes:

> We admit that in many places and in ordinary times the defendants in saying all that was said in the circular would have been within their constitutional rights. *But the character of every act depends upon the circumstances in which it is done.*

Referring to speech in wartime, the Court's opinion stated:

> When a nation is at war many things that might be said in time of peace are such a hindrance to its effort that their utterance will not be endured so long as men fight and that no Court could regard them as protected by any constitutional right.

The Supreme Court had had little to do with free speech cases because the First Amendment says: "Congress shall make no law . . . abridging the freedom of speech . . ." If a state law was involved it was not considered a matter for the high court. But in 1925, the Court declared that the Fourteenth Amendment to the Constitution protected free speech against violation by state laws. The Fourteenth Amendment, which had been passed after the

Oliver Wendell Holmes, Jr. (1841-1935), Associate Justice of the Supreme Court from 1902 till 1932. Known as the Great Dissenter, Holmes insisted that the Court interpret laws in the light of social change. He originated the clear and present danger test in free speech cases.

Civil War, stated in part ". . . nor shall any State deprive any person of life, liberty, or property, without due process of law . . ." In defining free speech as one of the liberties included in this amendment, the Supreme Court asserted its authority over all threats to freedom of expression, whether they should come from the federal or the state governments. From that time on the Court has sought the just limits to the question of free speech in a free society.

The United States Supreme Court, 1967. Back row: (left to right) Associate Justices Byron R. White, William J. Brennan, Jr., Potter Stewart, and Abe Fortas. Front row: Tom C. Clark (retired 1967), Hugo L. Black, Chief Justice Earl Warren, William O. Douglas, and John M. Harlan.

PART V

The Supreme Court Explores the Meaning of Free Speech

1. *Cases Heard by the Supreme Court*

The Chief Justice and eight Associate Justices of the Supreme Court are the guardians of the Constitution. They can make the final decision as to whether a law, or a ruling of a lower court, is depriving someone of his constitutional rights.

Very few cases originate in the Supreme Court. Most cases that come to the Supreme Court are appeals asking the Court to review, or reconsider, a decision made in a state court or in a lower federal court. In only a few kinds of situations is the Supreme Court compelled by law to hear and decide appealed cases. The Court may usually decide for itself whether the case is significant enough to be heard. Many cases do not get to the Supreme Court. This is either because they have not been appealed or because they were appealed but the Court decided not to hear the case.

2. *Freedom of Speech Cases Are a Special Problem*

When a case involving free speech is brought to the Supreme Court, it presents the justices with a difficult problem. The Court realizes that in a democracy freedom of speech must be protected as far as possible. It also realizes that government has the duty to protect the security of the nation. Communities must regulate traffic and protect their citizens against serious disturbances, such as riots. Sometimes, in attempting to protect the security of the nation, or to preserve peace and order, speech is limited. When this happens justices of the Supreme Court may be called upon to decide if the limitation was necessary and proper. They are learned men with vast knowledge of history and law. Like other human beings, however, their decisions are influenced by their own feelings about the proper limitations on speech, and they do not always agree with one another on a decision.

After the facts of a case have been discussed by members of the Court, a ruling is reached by a vote. Then a formal statement, called the opinion of the court, is prepared, giving the reasons for the decision. When all of the justices do not agree, both a majority and a minority, or dissenting, opinion may be prepared. In addition, any of the justices may write statements of their own about the case.

John Jay (1745-1829), first Chief Justice of the Supreme Court, and **John Marshall** (1755-1835), Chief Justice from 1801 to 1835. Marshall strengthened the Court, the Constitution, and the federal government in a series of important decisions. Without Marshall's guidance in its early years, the Court might have dwindled to insignificance.

Through the years the opinions of the Supreme Court have helped the people of the United States understand free speech by giving clear, thoughtful reasons for limiting or refusing to limit speech in a particular case. While majority opinion decides the case, minority opinions sometimes prove important historically. As conditions change, or as different men become members of the Court, the opinion that represented the thinking of the minority in one case sometimes becomes the opinion of the majority in another case.

3. *Tests Used by the Supreme Court*

To help decide cases involving freedom of speech, the justices of the Supreme Court have developed certain tests. Looking at some of the tests that have been used by the Court in the past cannot tell us how any case will be decided in the future. But it can show the kinds of thinking used by the Court in its search for the meaning of free speech.

4. *Clear and Present Danger Test*

Perhaps the most important test devised by the Supreme Court is the clear and present danger test. Although this test is rarely used by justices today, the idea it presents influences most Court thinking about free speech. The story of the clear and present danger test shows how ideas about free speech develop and change.

The words "clear and present danger" were first used by Justice Oliver Wendell Holmes in the Schenck case discussed in Part Four. At that time the test was the beginning of an idea that Justice Holmes had about certain words which become so dangerous under certain circumstances that the speaker who uses them is committing a crime. In the Schenck case, and in two other Espionage Act cases, Justice Holmes agreed with the other justices who voted that the defendants could be sent to jail because they had used speech which was intended to hurt the war effort and which could be dangerous to the security of the nation.

But in later cases the majority of the justices did not agree with Justice Holmes. He insisted that words were not illegal if there was time to prevent the danger that might be caused by those words. Justice Holmes believed that if people had time to think about ideas and to hear differing ideas, they would choose the truth and the danger feared would not occur.

One of those cases involved a group of young Russian immigrants who had printed some pamphlets on a small press and tossed them from the window of a New York building.

The pamphlets were written during World War I, when the United States was at war with Germany. They were not intended as a support of Germany. In fact, one of them stated: "We hate and despise German militarism more than you do hypocritical tyrants." The purpose of the leaflets was to protest the sending of American troops to Russia, where a revolution was taking place. However, they urged a general strike of munitions workers. If there had actually been a strike, Germany would have benefitted whether that had been the intention of the leaflets or not.

"Workers in the ammunition factories," the immigrants wrote, "you are producing bullets, bayonets, cannon to murder not only the Germans, but also your dearest, best, who are in Russia fighting for freedom." One of the leaflets ended with the words, "Workers, our reply to this barbaric intervention has to be a general strike."

Seven of the justices voted to uphold the conviction of the defendants. Justices Holmes and Louis D. Brandeis disagreed.

In the opinion of Justice Holmes, nobody could suppose that the publishing of a "silly leaflet by an unknown man," would present any immediate danger to the nation.

Justice Holmes said that if the words has been published with the intent of harming the United States, the defendants would have been guilty of a crime under the 1918 Sedition Act. But the intent was to stop American intervention in Russia, and this was not a crime.

Justice Holmes explained that clear and present danger meant that the expression of ideas should be checked only when they threaten a danger so immediate and so great that action would have to be taken at once to save the country.

Eight years after Justice Holmes first announced the clear and present danger test, Justice Brandeis wrote an opinion, with the agreement of Justice Holmes, that carried it still further. Brandeis said that even words which threaten to cause immediate danger cannot justify the prohibition of speech unless the danger feared is relatively serious. "The fact that speech is likely to result in some violence or destruction of property is not enough to justify suppression," he said. "There must be the probability of serious injury to the State."

Justices Oliver Wendell Holmes and Louis D. Brandeis planted ideas about freedom of speech which were not accepted by the majority of their fellow members of the high court. But the ideas lived and gradually gained Court support after the death of Holmes and shortly before the retirement of Brandeis.

Louis D. Brandeis (1856-1941), Associate Justice of the Supreme Court from 1916 until 1939. As a lawyer, Brandeis had supported social reform, and his appointment to the Court was bitterly opposed in the Senate. With Holmes he developed and expanded the clear and present danger test in free speech cases.

5. Dangerous Tendency

While Justices Holmes and Brandeis argued time and again for the clear and present danger test, the majority of the Court favored a test known as the dangerous tendency test. The Court asked: Could the words of the speaker or writer be dangerous because they might start some action that could lead to danger to the public peace or national security?

Starting in 1925, the Court decided it could hear free speech cases arising out of laws passed by state legislatures. Prior to then the court believed that the individual states were the best judges of what they must do to protect themselves and their citizens.

6. Preferred Position

By 1943, after both Justices Holmes and Brandeis were dead, the Supreme Court was made up of justices with a majority favoring the clear and present danger test.

The Court was then using the theory known as preferred position for cases involving freedom of expression. Preferred position was the idea that it was the duty of the Court to protect First Amendment freedoms over other rights because they are essentials of a free society. It was not one specific test but it did use Justice Brandeis' idea that speech should be regulated only under emergency situations, or when *serious evil would immediately result to an important social interest* if the speech in question was permitted.

For almost 10 years after 1940, freedom of speech was held by the Court to be in a preferred position. Even during World War II, people were free to speak their differing opinions without fear of arrest. The Espionage Act of 1917 was (and is) still on the books. Only one case under this act came before the Supreme Court as a result of speech used during World War II, and the clear and present danger test was used to reverse the conviction. The American people found that allowing freedom of speech to those who disagreed with the policies of the government did not harm the war effort.

Senator Joseph R. McCarthy addresses a crowd in Platteville, Wisconsin. During the years 1950 to 1954 McCarthy investigated communist influence in government, education, and industry. Most of his charges were unfounded, but he succeeded in arousing fear and in limiting the freedom to express political opinions.

7. *Serious Future Danger*

By 1950 a growing concern about international communism had spread throughout the United States. As in the days of the Sedition Act of 1798 and as in World War I, this concern caused the American people to want to limit speech they felt was dangerous. A majority of the justices began to think that the clear and present danger test could not be applied to speech which urged the overthrow of the government. Instead of requiring present danger, the Court used a test which would allow speech to be limited if the words spoken or written were likely to result in serious danger in the future.

The Court, using the serious future danger test, would permit Congress or state legislatures to prohibit speech which favored the overthrow of the U.S. Government by force and which actually taught methods of overthrowing the government to be used whenever the time was right. The Court felt that in this case the danger is serious even though a revolution might only happen sometime in the distant future. Most of the justices thought that it was not possible to apply the clear and present danger test to speech which urged the overthrow of the government by force and violence. By the time the danger was serious and immediate it would be too late to save the country.

8. *The Court Today*

No matter what test a particular court uses, the Supreme Court is agreed that speech must sometimes be limited under the following circumstances:

1. When it presents a danger to national security.
2. When it threatens to disturb peace and order.
3. When the speaker urges his audience to commit a crime and the audience is so worked up that it appears likely they will follow his urging.

However, any particular case may bring up questions which the justices do not always agree on. These questions are:

1. Is there really a danger?
2. How great should the *chance* of danger be before officials limit the speaker's right to express himself and the listener's right to hear?
3. Should speech which might cause a minor danger be limited, or should it be limited only if the danger feared is serious?

Thurgood Marshall, appointed to the Supreme Court in 1967, has served on the U. S. Court of Appeals and as solicitor general of the United States. From 1938 to 1961 he was chief counsel for the NAACP and in 1954 presented the case for school desegregation before the Supreme Court.

9. *The Case of Feiner versus New York*

This actual case heard in 1951 is an excellent example of many points discussed in this chapter.

The facts of the case

A university student named Feiner, standing on a box and speaking over loudspeakers mounted on a car, made a speech on a street corner in Syracuse, New York. About 75 people, some Negro and some white, crowded around him so that people wishing to pass had to go onto the highway.

During his speech, Feiner called President Truman a "bum" and the American Legion "a Nazi Gestapo." He accused the mayor of Syracuse, whom he called a "champagne-sipping bum," of not speaking for the Negro people. Some members of the crowd became excited when Feiner said: "The Negroes don't have equal rights; they should rise up in arms and fight for them." One man said that if the police didn't get Feiner off the stand, he would do so himself.

Two policemen who witnessed the scene said there was angry muttering and pushing in the crowd and they were afraid a riot would break out. When Feiner continued to speak after the police-men twice told him to stop, he was arrested.

Feiner's case was first heard in a New York trial court where he was found guilty of disorderly conduct. The trial judge felt that the policemen were justified in arresting Feiner to prevent a breach of the peace.

Feeling that his constitutional right to free speech had been violated, Feiner appealed his case to the New York court of appeals, which upheld the conviction.

Then Feiner appealed to the New York State Supreme Court, and again the conviction was upheld.

University students gather to hear speeches for and against the war in Viet Nam.

Finally Feiner appealed to the United States Supreme Court. A majority of the justices voted to uphold the judgment of the lower court. Chief Justice Vinson, speaking for the majority, pointed out that Feiner was not arrested for making the speech or for the ideas he expressed. The Court recognized his right to use loudspeaking equipment and to say what he did about President Truman, the Mayor of Syracuse, and the American Legion. However, Vinson said, Feiner expressed his views in a way which would cause a danger of riot, and for that reason his arrest was constitutional.

The majority opinion by Chief Justice Fred M. Vinson

The courts below recognized petitioner's (Feiner's) right to hold a street meeting at this locality, to make use of loud-speaking equipment in giving his speech, and to make derogatory remarks concerning public officials and the American Legion. They found that the officers in making the arrest were motivated solely by a proper concern for the preservation of order and protection of the general welfare, and that there was no evidence which could lend color to a claim that the acts of the police were a cover for suppression of petitioner's views and opinions. Petitioner was thus neither arrested nor convicted for the making or the content of his speech. Rather it was the reaction which it actually engendered.

. . . When clear and present danger of riot, disorder, interference with traffic upon the public streets, or other immediate threat to public safety, peace, or order, appears, the power of the State to prevent or punish is obvious.

. . . ordinary murmurings and objections of a hostile audience cannot be allowed to silence a speaker, and we are also mindful of the possible danger of giving overzealous police officials complete discretion to break up otherwise lawful public meetings. But we are not faced here with

such a situation. It is one thing to say that the police cannot be used as an instrument for the suppression of unpop-
ular views, and another to say that, when as here the speaker
passes the bounds of argument or persuasion and under-
takes incitement to riot, they are powerless to prevent a
breach of peace . . .

Fred M. Vinson (1890-1953), Chief Justice of the Supreme Court
from 1946 to 1953. The Vinson court often reflected the nation's
widespread fear of communism during the decade following World
War II. In free speech cases, many decisions were based upon the
serious future danger test.

Justice Black dissents

. . . The police of course have power to prevent breaches of the peace. But if, in the name of preserving order, they ever can interfere with a lawful public speaker, they first must make all reasonable efforts to protect him. . . . According to the officers' testimony, the crowd was restless but there is no showing of any attempt to quiet it; pedestrians were forced to walk into the street, but there was no effort to clear a path on the sidewalk; one person threatened to assault petitioner but the officers did nothing to discourage this when even a word might have sufficed. Their duty was to protect petitioner's right to talk, even to the extent of arresting the man who threatened to interfere. . . .

Justice Douglas, joined by Justice Minton, writes separate dissenting opinion

A speaker may not, of course, incite a riot any more than he may incite a breach of the peace by the use of "fighting words". . . . But this record shows no such extremes. It shows an unsympathetic audience and the threat of one man to haul the speaker from the stage. It is against that kind of threat that speakers need police protection. If they do not receive it and instead the police throw their weight on the side of those who would break up the meetings, the police become the new censors of speech. . . .

University students sign a petition to support American participation in the Viet Nam war.

PART VI

Some Specific Rights

Absolute freedom of speech, which would be the freedom to say anything, anywhere, at any time, does not exist. You cannot commit a crime with words and claim protection under the first amendment. For example, you cannot use words to threaten someone or to offer a bribe. Limits may be placed on speech to protect peace and order and national security. In spite of the limits, Americans have a great deal of freedom to express their ideas.

1. *What You Can Do Under Your Right to Free Speech*

1. You may stand on a street corner and make a speech giving your ideas about religion, government, law, or any other subject. The police will protect your right to express your ideas. However, if the crowd that gathers around you is so huge it spills out into the streets, stopping traffic or causing a danger of accidents, the police may ask you to move.

2. You are free to pass out handbills or pamphlets giving your views from a street corner or a public park. You do not need to get a permit to do this so long as your pamphlets or handbills are expressions of your views and not advertisements for a commercial product or project.

3. You may make a speech in a public park, but you might be required to get a license or permit to do so. Whether the license is granted or refused should depend only on questions of traffic, normal use of the park, and public safety. A permit could be refused, for example, because the park you want to speak in is normally used for Little League ball games which would be interfered with by your speech making. If a certain park is not available for the time you want to make your speech, you can get a license for another time or place. The license or permit cannot be refused because of anything you are going to say in your speech.

4. If you want to speak directly to people in their homes about your religion or your favorite candidate during an election, you may ring their doorbells and ask them to hear what you have to say. You may also leave pamphlets or handbills inside of their doors, but not in their mailbox. If the resident does not want his doorbell rung he must post a sign by the bell with this information on it.

Silent vigil. A group gathers near the Armory on the University
of Minnesota campus. Minneapolis, February 1967.

Political discussion on a street corner. Police may intervene if the
crowd creates a traffic hazard.

Thousands of people from all over the United States took part in the civil rights march in Washington, D. C., August 28, 1963. The purpose of the march was to demonstrate support for passage of the Civil Rights Bill.

5. You may get a group together to parade through the streets of your city carrying signs of protest, speaking, singing, or chanting. You will probably be required to get a license for the parade. As with all other licenses involving free speech, this one will be granted or denied only on questions of safety and traffic. No licensing official can deny you a license because he doesn't like the ideas you are expressing.

Martin Luther King, Jr., civil rights leader. King's nonviolent methods of protest are protected by the First Amendment.

6. You may express ideas that you know the audience will not like. If the audience becomes angry and threatens to stop you, the police will *usually* protect your right to speak and attempt to keep order among the audience. However, if the audience becomes so angry that police do not think they can control it, you will be asked to stop speaking and probably punished if you do not stop when asked.

7. You can make a speech or pass out pamphlets which attempt to show that communism, socialism, fascism, or any other form of government is better than democracy. This is not a crime unless you actually urge the overthrow of the American government by force and violence, or suggest ways to overthrow it by force and violence.

George Lincoln Rockwell, leader of the American Nazi Party, speaks at the University of Minnesota. Rockwell was assassinated by a member of his own group in August 1967.

The Ku Klux Klan, first organized as a social group for southern veterans of the Civil War, has died and reappeared several times in the past century. The Klan's activities — usually directed against Negroes — are often violent and destructive, but its rights to assemble and to speak are guarded by the First Amendment.

2. *What You Cannot Do Under the Right to Free Speech*

1. You cannot use "fighting words" in a speech you are making. That is, you cannot say such insulting things about a member of the audience that a fight is likely to break out as a result.

2. You cannot speak in a park or organize a parade if you have been denied a license, even if you think the license was denied illegally. If, in your opinion, the license was denied for any reason besides the availability of the space you requested, poor timing, or a bad traffic situation, you may seek help from the courts.

3. In communities which have "Race Hate" or "Group Libel" laws, you may not make a speech or pass out handbills or pamphlets attacking or ridiculing a particular race, religion, or organization.

4. You cannot make a speech or pass out printed materials in a privately owned place such as a restaurant, hotel, department store, or theater lobby unless you have permission of the management.

5. In speaking, or in printed materials, you cannot urge the audience to commit a crime. For example, you can make a speech in which you criticize the poor garbage collection in your city, but you might get arrested if you told your audience to throw garbage on the mayor's lawn.

6. You cannot say or write things about a person which will damage that person's reputation and cause him to suffer in either his business or personal life. Neither can you say or write things which will blacken the memory of a dead person.

If the words are spoken the crime is *slander*. If the words are written the crime is *libel*. To commit slander the insulting words have to be spoken to someone other than the person you are talking about. If you make the damaging remarks directly to the person you are talking about, they are considered slander if at least one person overhears.

However, you have a great deal of freedom to express your criticism of candidates for public office or persons holding public office. Here the interest of the public is more important than the interest of the official and you will not be guilty of libel or slander unless it is obvious that you are deliberately lying.

7. Although you can protest against the draft and the United States' participation in a war, you can be arrested if you teach men how to use false methods to keep from being drafted.

8. In making a speech, printing a pamphlet or handbill, or carrying a protest sign, you cannot use obscene language.

ag-burning in Central
ark, New York City, 1967.
this means of protest also
uarded by the First
mendment?

Counter-demonstrators (above) gather along the route of the protest march against the war in Viet Nam. New York City, April 15, 1967.

. . . INDEX . . .

ACKNOWLEDGMENTS

The illustrations are reproduced through the courtesy of: pp. 6, Beddow, 10, Cummins, 49, Zerby, 53 and 55 (top), Roscoe, 57 (bottom), Erskine, from the Minnesota Daily, University of Minnesota; pp. 7, 31 (top), 37, 44, 51, Library of Congress; pp. 8, 9, 14, 15, 18, 20, 23, 34, 35 (bottom), 40 (right), 55 (bottom), 57 (top), 58, Independent Picture Service; p. 11, Minneapolis Star and Tribune; p. 16, Virginia Museum of Fine Arts; p. 21, Curators of the Bodleian Library, Oxford University; p. 22, New York Public Library, Astor, Lenox and Tilden Foundations; p. 27, U. S. Navy; p. 28, Museum of Fine Arts, Boston; p. 29, Amherst College; p. 31 (bottom), Walters Art Gallery; p. 33, Chicago Historical Society; p. 35 (top), American Civil Liberties Union; p. 39, Harris & Ewing; p. 40 (left), Metropolitan Museum of Art; p. 46, State Historical Society of Wisconsin; p. 48, National Association for the Advancement of Colored People; p. 56, NBC Photo; pp. 59, 60, ABC News.

ABOUT THE AUTHOR . . .

RAVINA GELFAND graduated from the University of Minnesota where she studied English, journalism, and psychology. She also did postgraduate work in English and writing at both the University and Macalester College. A former weekly newspaper editor, she has written for radio and magazines and is the co-author of *They Wouldn't Quit: Stories of Handicapped People*. Her husband, Louis I. Gelfand, is on the Board of Directors of the Minnesota affiliate, American Civil Liberties Union. They live in Minneapolis with their two sons.

The IN AMERICA *Series*

We specialize in publishing quality books for young people. For a complete list please write:

Lerner Publications Company
241 First Avenue North, Minneapolis, Minnesota 55401